ESSENTIALS FOR SUCCULENT GARDENING

The Complete Guide to Gardening, Growing, Caring, Preventing and Cure for Diseases for Your Succulent Plant

By

Adams Ross

BY   ADAMS ROSS

TABLE OF CONTENTS

- Propagation

CHAPTER FOUR:

- Succulent Diseases and Problems: Solutions to Your Plant's Symptoms

CHAPTER 1

Planning and Designing Your Garden

Professional landscape designers keep certain considerations in mind as they evaluate a site. When you understand these fundamentals, beautiful gardens will no longer seem mysterious and unattainable. You will view your own garden afresh and be better able to implement—and communicate—what you hope to achieve. This chapter explains how basic design principles apply to yards, pathways, slopes, and more, and it shows the aesthetic applications of a wide variety of succulents. As you prepare your garden's canvas, continually envision the placement of plants that appeal to you. You will soon recognize those that are especially useful and begin to realize how they might enhance your landscape. Soft leaved Agave attenuate, for example, is among the most appealing and versatile of plants—and a key component of many of the gardens shown in this book.

SUN CONSIDERATIONS

Throughout the year, the sun rises and sets at gradually earlier or later times and at slightly different spots on the horizon. These seasonal changes affect the quantity of light, heat, and shade that your house, outdoor living spaces, and garden receive. In general, slopes that drop to the north or northeast get less heat than those that fall to the south or southwest. Landscape architects often place swimming pools on the west side of homes because people use their pools in the afternoon and want to enjoy the sunset while relaxing in the spa or dining outdoors. In addition to helping to determine areas of outdoor activity, sunlight factors into optimal growing conditions for plants. In southern latitudes, for example, heat sensitive aeronauts and it need full sun in winter and semi shade in summer. In high elevation or desert gardens, where the sun is harsh, they will need some shade.

In lower elevations in northern latitudes, those same plants will do fine in full summer sun. Plants in any region tend to grow in the direction of greatest sun exposure. Rosette and fountain shaped succulents do this noticeably, and their placement in the garden should be made with this in mind. In my sloping, east facing garden, for example, a large Agave Americana 'Marginata' grows just east of a pathway but does not encroach, because it leans toward the morning sun. Orient new plants—especially large ones—in the direction they would grow in nature or their placement will appear contrived. The elements also impact a garden's aesthetics. Sunlight cast on spiny plants makes them glow and creates intriguing shadows. Silhouettes and the sky are part of a landscape, as is the wind, which creates motion. Feathery ornamental grasses and narrow leaved succulents, such as Yucca whipped and days liaisons, are living mobiles; they shimmer when backlit and ripple in the breeze. And any garden benefits from the addition of water—even if only suggested by a dry streambed.

PREPARE AND REPAIR

During your garden's planning stages, sketch its layout on graph paper. Begin by drawing anything that will not change, such as your house, property boundaries, walls, and fences. Make several copies of the basic sketch, and then use them to conceptualize different garden plans. One plan might have straight pathways aligned on a central axis, perhaps with a fountain in the middle; another might have paths that flow around a pond or peninsula shaped beds. Keep in mind views, microclimates, and practical considerations such as utilities and tool storage. Sketch walkways that lead to and connect outdoor areas for sitting, sunning, dining, and other activities tailored to your family's needs and recreational interests. Next, plan the layout of each garden room, defining where various elements—such as large rocks, decking, outdoor furnishings, and container groupings—will go. Represent trees as circles that approximate their size at maturity, and use colored pencils to block in massed plantings. Shaggy trees can be transformed with proper trimming. Once established, a tree cannot be moved—or removed—without expense and inconvenience, so before you plant one, find out how large it will grow, how much leaf litter it will shed, and whether it is prone to disease. Depending on where a tree is positioned, it can shade a sunny window or sitting area; cut glare from water, reflective buildings, or pavement; and deflect (or redirect) wind. If you want shade in summer and sun in winter, plant deciduous trees. Many excellent books explain how to build berms, terraces, and retaining walls and install pathways, irrigation systems, and outdoor lighting. One comprehensive guide for homeowners is Complete Home Landscaping, by Catriona Tudor Erler (2000). If your concept is especially complex, design software programs can help. For any task beyond your expertise, such as installing apergola, deck, patio, pool, or other water feature—or tackling drainage and other grading concerns—hire a professional. Most landscape professionals charge an hourly fee and can provide an estimate on an entire project, from initial plans to installation. If you see a garden you like, ask the property owner who helped create and/or install it. Also check with horticultural societies, garden clubs, the local Cactus and Succulent Society of America (CSSA) chapter, and nurseries that specialize in dry climate plants. Organizations such as the American Association of Landscape Architects (ASLA) and, in California, the California Landscape Contractors Association (CLCA) can provide names of members in your area. Request to see past projects—not just photos, but actual gardens you can visit. Rapport is important; make sure the landscaper shares your aesthetic, welcomes your input, has worked with succulents, and understands their cultivation requirements.

EVALUATE THE SOIL

Unlike roses and tropicals, succulents do not require a growing medium so rich in organic matter it resembles chocolate cake. But should your garden be blessed with such soil, succulents likely will thrive if it provides the drainage they require. Determine your soil type by digging a whole the size of a 1 gallon nursery pot. Then fill the hole with water. If it drains rapidly, in a few minutes or less, your soil is probably sandy, which will benefit from the addition of organic matter. If the water takes an hour or more to drain, the soil likely is clay and inhospitable to succulents—indeed, to most garden plants—and you will need to amend the soil, build raised beds, or make planting berms that contain a good growing medium. Public gardens that cultivate succulents formulate their amendments based on deficiencies in the native soil. At the Santa Barbara Botanic Garden, for example, heavy clay soil is amended with compost, gravel, sharp sand, and wood chips—a mix designed more to enhance texture than nutrient content. (Sharp sand, unlike fine, silty sand, has coarse grains that feel sharp when rubbed between the Fingertips.) At the Huntington Botanical Gardens in San Marino, California, forest compost is added to the soil, plus pumice if drainage needs improvement, prior to planting. At the Arizona Sonora Desert Museum in Tucson, which showcases cacti, heavy soil is top dressed with 6 to 12 inches of well draining soil mixed with enough sulfur to keep the pH between 6.5 and 8. Obviously, since soil varies from region to region, and even within areas of a garden, amendment formulas vary. The only definitive method to find out which additives—such as agricultural lime and compost—will turn your soil into the perfect growing medium is to have it analyzed. This also will determine its alkalinity (a pH between 6 and 7 is best for succulents).

WATER AND IRRIGATION

If you are planning a landscape of primarily desert adapted plants and larger agaves and aloes, you may not need to irrigate your garden if rainfall is adequate. The plants should be fine with infrequent watering with a hose and detachable sprinklers. But just because cacti and succulents can survive without irrigation does not mean they do not appreciate it. A little extra water can make the difference between a parched landscape and a green and lush garden. When succulents are actively growing, they do best when watered well once or twice a week. As they enter dormancy, they need less water—on average, every two to three weeks. The majority of succulents are winter dormant, but a few slow down in summer. In this book, if a particular plant will suffer when watered during its dormancy, that fact is noted in the Plant Palette. Most succulents can handle more water than they need, providing their roots are in coarse, fast draining soil. Although this means you can mix them with ornamentals that have greater water requirements, the best companions for succulents need a minimal amount once established.

To take advantage of natural drainage, position succulents on the tops and sides of berms and banks, so they are higher than their thirstier neighbors. Perennials and annuals that need more water should go at the base of such a planting, where runoff is greatest. If you live in a hot, dry climate, you will find an in ground, automatic irrigation system a great convenience. Automatic systems (which also can be used manually) can be programmed according to zone, so that a lawn receives more water than, say, a bank of ice plants. Minimize water waste with micro sprayers, bubblers, low angle nozzles, and drip irrigation. Drip puts water where a plant needs it most and cuts down on weed growth from overspray. Drip emitters dribble steadily and can be retrofitted into conventional systems.

Use screw on adapters to extend drip tubing from the nearest riser to the base of a plant. Impact sprinklers and fixed or pop up spray heads are the most popular irrigation products for watering lawns, slopes, and densely planted areas. Spray heads provide options in terms of how much area they cover (full circle, half circle, quarter circle, or a horizontal strip) and the volume of water they project. Because spray heads can be easily changed, you can mix or switch them to serve greater or lesser areas. After your irrigation system is installed, test it seasonally to evaluate its efficiency.

BASICS OF GARDEN DESIGN

As you delve into the six main elements of design, you will gain clarity on how to create an aesthetically pleasing landscape that perfectly meets your needs. Elements detailed here are scale and proportion, repetition, contrast, emphasis, and texture. The last element, color, is so useful in maximizing the design potential of succulents; the entire next chapter is devoted to it. Scale and proportion Scale and proportion concern the size of plants and structures in the landscape as they relate to one another and to the whole. A landscape with properly proportioned elements feels inviting and is a good fit for its human inhabitants. For example, a large tree that dwarfs a small house would look more proportional alongside a multistory building. A 3 foot pond that suits a small yard would be practically invisible in a large park. Correct scale and proportion can be as simple as placing small plants in small spaces and large plants in large spaces. It is more effective to fill a blank wall or corner with a single dasylirion—or a large ornamental pot—instead of a jumble of geraniums. Intimate areas lend themselves to frilly echeverias and jewel like sedums; large areas, to majestic agaves, yuccas, aloes, and companion plants such as phormiums. If your back yard feels open and unprotected, the right sized plants can transform it into a sheltered open air room.

Conversely, an area of your yard that feels claustrophobic likely will benefit from removing clutter and pruning to open up trees and shrubs Repetition. The foliage of a plant is often more important in garden design than its brief floral display. Perhaps more than any other plants, succulents—because their leaf shapes are distinctly pointed, oval, or cylindrical—offer opportunities for crisply defined repetitions of form. Designers refer to these harmonious, recurring patterns as a garden's rhythms. They have the same soothing effect as a musical motif; in fact, when I see such repetitions in a well designed garden, I hear music. Repetition can be a difficult principle for plant collectors who want one of everything and see no point in having extras. But repetition is essential for unifying a landscape. Large agaves, in particular, illustrate this: Just three of them, all the same and strategically placed, will lend continuity to a garden, regardless of its other components. And if those agaves are variegated, so much the better; their striped leaves will provide another motif.

Repetition is not always multiples of the same plant, though. It can be achieved in subtle ways, by creating patterns and using silhouettes. A yucca planted near an agave shares the same spiky shape, as do tufts of blue fescue at its base. Color, too, is an effective way of playing the same tune with multiple instruments. Combine Seneca serpents, Agave parry, Crassula arborescence, and Fistula glace, and you have four part harmony sung in silvery blue. Contrast Repetition is soothing, contrast is exciting, and a well designed garden has both. Repetition works up to a point and then becomes tedious; this is when contrast comes into play. For example, in a multiple planting of agaves and yuccas, the addition of soft, airy ornamental grasses is refreshing. Or you might add a plant that contrasts with the agaves' blue gray color, such as red or coral colored Kalanchoes blossfeldiana or bright red Crassula coccinea 'Campfi re'. Asymmetry is another form of contrast and can be used effectively to lend interest to a monotonous landscape. Although symmetry—such as urns planted with aeronauts flanking an entryway, or a driveway bordered on both sides with aloes—can be pleasing because of repetition, few plants in nature form perfect pairs or grow in straight lines. Asymmetry, like curves, is more natural. Anything aligned, straight, or right angled suggests human intervention.

Spiky leaves on a slender Dracaena Marginata repeat the outline of Agave tequila, while the blue of the agave echoes the color of the home's window frame. Stephen Hill garden, San Diego. Design by Southwest Landscape

Coral tree (Erythrina ×sykesii) flowers repeat the orange of Aloe ferox spires. In the background is yellow blooming marlothii.

Drifts of blue senecio match the trim color of this home, as do the leaves of Aloe ferox (foreground, with orange red flowers spikes). At upper left is an Aloe barbered tree; on the right, Alluaudia procera. Janice Byrne garden, Del Mar, CA. Design by Bill Teague

A peach colored wall repeats the sunset hue of Euphoria BIA tirucalli 'Sticks on Fire', which in turn contrasts with the gray blue ornamental grass and Cotyledon Orbiculata (lower right). Threadlike grass stems are echoed by the larger baseball bat branches of the tall euphorbia and

Again, by the chopstick limbs of 'Sticks on Fire'. Shapes contrast: The euphorbia in the background is tall and slender, 'Sticks on Fire' is midsized and shrubby, and Festuca glauca forms a low mass of up thrusting points.

Design by owner Suzy Schaefer

Aconitum arboreum 'Zwartkop', shown here in full bloom, contrasts with the home's pale hues and white trim.

Wispy Mexican feather grass (Nassella tenuissima) pro vides a delightful texture contrast to agaves. Unlike more thirsty ornamental grasses, its cultivation requirements are similar to those of succulents. Don and Jill Young gar den, San Diego. Design by owners and Bill Schnetz, Schnetz Landscape, Inc.

Emphasis

Emphasis refers to any item strategically placed to attract attention, such as a tree, statue, or fountain used as a focal point. These draw people toward garden areas and create destinations. Obvious locales to emphasize are the center of a circle or the end of an allée. Less obvious are a bend in a curving pathway or a gap in a hedge. Hardscape creates sight lines that lead the eye to what lies beyond. If you live on a slope overlooking a golf course, city skyline, distant mountains, the ocean, or a verdant canyon, position sitting and entertaining areas accordingly and frame the view with large and majestic agaves or cereus. Also, consider your home's windows as picture frames and create outdoor garden vignettes you can enjoy from indoors. Another useful landscaping concept, the axis, is a visual line that extends between two emphasized elements, such as a walkway that connects two sitting areas. In formal gardens, plants typically are aligned on either side of an axis, and focal points are placed where two axes intersect. Because sight lines can also emphasize undesirable objects, evaluate your landscape for unattractive items you have seen so often, you no longer see them. One way to gain fresh perspective on your garden is to turn your back on it and look at its reflection in a hand mirror. When I did that in my own yard, I noticed a yellow "Yield" sign on the busy street beyond. Before I saw it reflected in the mirror, I had been oblivious to the sign. When you identify an eyesore, take measures to make it less obvious. Either position something intriguing in the same line of sight, so the viewer's eye stops there, or camoufl age the offending object with shrubs or a structure, such as a lattice screen. If the problem is a telephone pole, a vertical plant will hide it or draw the eye away from it. Should you want to veil neighboring second story windows, add lacy trees that have similar cultivation requirements as succulents but that are much faster growing—such as Melaleuca and Acacia. Multiple plantings of yuccas, Euphorbia tirucalli, large aloes, and agaves can also serve as living walls, screens, and hedge Magazine stylists, prior to a photo shoot, routinely remove or disguise anything in a garden that strikes a discordant note and calls unwanted attention to itself.

Typically, these include garden hoses, plastic pots, dirty or faded patio umbrellas, and anything leaning at an odd angle (such as bamboo torches). As I prepared my own garden to be photographed, I made utility boxes disappear by painting them the same color as the stucco wall behind them; hid a hose in a wooden barrel (I threaded the hose through a knothole in the bottom); spray painted white irrigation risers brown or replaced them (they come in black and gray); and painted a tool shed the same tan color as my garden's soil. Texture is integral to other elements of design and refers to the way light hits surfaces. Texture is both visual and tactile. Use it to enhance contrast and repetition and to call attention to focal points. Keep it in mind as you select and position plants that have fuzzy, waxy, shiny, or dull leaves. Other textural aspects of a garden include tree bark, hard cape, and the overall shapes and forms of shrubs— which can change depending on whether they are viewed up close or from a distance. Textural effect is relative to the surroundings.

Even gravel, which at first appears coarse, can look soft when placed alongside boulders. Designers like to mix textures to create striking contrasts, but a little goes a long way. The addition of plants with midsized leaves can serve as an effective bridge. Three dasylirion with pincushion silhouettes contrast beautifully with the soft cloud of feathery green foliage on a Mexican Palo verde (Parkinsonia aculeata). Euphorbia cooperi, at left, adds a thicker texture. Christopher and Jodi Queen garden, San Diego Spiky Yucca rostra

GARDEN ENHANCEMENTS

As you conceptualize your landscape, consider incorporating a water feature, a structure, or a similar enhancement that makes your garden an inviting extension of your home. Water features Splashing water blankets intrusive sounds and muffles conversations, so even your closest neighbors cannot overhear. It also mirrors the sky, creates a habitat for fish, and serves as a focal point. Options include birdbaths, free standing fountains, in ground ponds, and recirculating streams. The soothing sound of a waterfall enhances Thomas Hobbs's Vancouver garden. The water feature's stone walls shelter a collection of echeverias and green and white–leaved Sedum spectabile 'Frosty Morn'. Design by owner Thomas Hobbs. Photo by Allan Mandell A pond, fountain, and potted cycad grace the entry garden of a Rancho Santa Fe estate. Pavers laid on the diagonal make the space seem larger. Aloe plicatilis in the foreground adds color and texture.

Structures and hardscapes an arbor lend height and vertical interest and can support a flowering vine, such as hoya, or an edible one, such as grapes. Such structures also might shelter a bench or a table and chairs. Pathways lead visitors to various garden destinations and serve as roadways for anything with wheels—from tricycles to wheelbarrows. Pavement options include bricks, randomly placed flagstones, stepping stones, gravel, and poured concrete. When positioned outside a sliding glass door, a patio or deck provides an easily accessible dining and sitting area. Situated in the garden—perhaps alongside a pool or barbecue grill—patios and decks define outdoor rooms. Planters and raised beds lend themselves to herb and vegetable gardens and can show off cascading succulents, such as graptopetalums and burro tail (Sedum morganianum).

If you have small children, set aside areas for a lawn, sandbox, and/or swing set. Bright colored plastic jungle gyms and playhouses can be eyesores, so do not position them prominently—a side yard is ideal. To transform a patio or garden room into an inviting area at night, install a fire pit or outdoor fi replace. Use river rocks and gravel that channel rainwater to suggest an arroyo (dry creek bed) and provide a natural looking access area for maintenance.

FRONT YARD IDEAS

Traditional front yard landscapes tend to be bland and high maintenance, with turf that needs mowing, fertilizing, and de thatching. Lawns are often bordered by shrubs that need pruning and beds planted with annuals. One or more trees drop leaves that require raking. No green component will survive without regular and ample water. Envision, instead, a meandering pathway of brick or stone that connects the sidewalk to your front door. Flanking it are mounds of decomposed granite dotted with boulders and planted with aeronauts, agaves, echeverias, and tree aloes. Ice plants and ornamental grasses provide contrasting colors and textures. In general, a garden of succulents and drought tolerant ornamentals needs one to two thirds less water than the same area of lawn. A lawn requires more water per square foot than anything else you might grow in the same space. It is an ideal play surface for children, but for most activities, 500 to 800 square feet is plenty. A reduced size lawn will be more visually appealing if it flows in graceful curves rather than being square or rectangular. You might flank an oval lawn with a dormant he mum that blooms vivid pink or red in spring and that surrounds several dramatic variegated agaves. Moreover, a lawn, because it needs mowing, has to be level (or nearly so). When you replace it, you have the option of creating highs and lows that suggest hills and valleys. Mounded soil is more visually interesting, adds instant height to young trees, and discourages people from cutting across newly planted areas.

Pathways between mounds might lead to tucked away sitting areas as well as your home's entry. Michael Buckner, owner of The Plant Man nursery in San Diego, specializes in converting turf and flower bed yards to succulent landscapes. He says it takes only three years for a newly planted succulent garden to fill in; by five years, it looks so good that people assume it has been there twenty. Buckner begins designing front yards by considering the location of the street and mailbox, where people open their car doors, and where they park. In his landscapes, the front yard is wide and inviting. He adds boulders, believing they lend a sense of mystery and beckon the viewer to explore beyond. He brings in soil is that is amended with pumice, so it drains well, and then positions mounds of soil and boulders according to the highs and lows of the home. If a house has a gable on the left, for example, he places the largest boulder on the opposite side for balance. The biggest rock is placed first, as in a painting. Large and upright succulents come next, and then smaller ones. He also plants in drifts, because in nature, plants grow naturally where water distributes itself over the landscape.

PATHWAY PLANTINGS

Pathways through a succulent garden provide a means for people to enjoy aeronauts, aloes, echeveria, and more up close. For a simple, eye catching juxtaposition of complementary colors, flank orange hued pavers with blue senecio.

STREETSIDE GARDENS

When landscaping a street side garden, consider
the scale of the area to be filled and provide hard
cape if the area will have foot traffic. To create a
simple but harmonious composition, repeat plant
material and arrange ground covers in swaths. If
you install large agaves and aloes, make sure they
have plenty of room to grow, so they will not need
trimming

SLOPES AND TERRACES

Steep terrain can be challenging to landscape, but
it can be fun to explore a garden that you must
ascend or descend, especially one that reveals
something new at each switchback. When you sit,
you are enveloped in greenery, yet you also enjoy
the view.

One approach is to cover a slope with ice plants
and ignore it—which is what the previous owners
of my own garden chose to do. For years, much of

the 30   degree slope behind my home was blanketed with Dorsa the mum

Floribunda, which bloomed bright purple in spring and, along with oaks, held the soil against erosion. I did not view the terrain as usable land until I created a succulent

This quintessential Southern California landscape showcases readily available succulents and companion plants. Blue gray clusters of Agave Americana echo drifts of Seneca mantra lascar (foreground). Red bougainvillea adds color in summer and autumn; Aloe arborescence blooms in winter and spring. Rosemary provides green mounding shrubs, with Canary Island date palms and California pepper trees lending contrasting texture and height.

The solution was to dig an fl at, semicircular area into the bottom of the slope. Low walls of pressure treated wood retain the bank, and existing trees shade the area and create a natural roof for the outdoor room. In the bank around the top of the retaining wall, I planted succulents that have filled in and cascade: aeronauts, sedums, and kalian chose. The result is an inviting outdoor room and a sitting area surrounded by a half wreath of succulents. Every slope is different and presents its own challenges, but the basic approach to landscaping a hillside is to build retaining walls to form terraces, and then connect these with pathways and steps.

If you have a steep front yard that slopes down to a sidewalk, you might build a retaining wall at the base of the bank. The wall will define your yard and serve as a raised bed for flower, shrubs, and ground covers. The higher the wall, the less steep the slope will be. Also consider mortar less retaining walls. These have built in drainage, because moisture seeps between the stones, creating an environment for naturally cliff dwelling sedums, achiever as , Dudley's, and simper vivums.

Make sure any retaining wall can withstand pressure exerted on it by the slope it holds back. During construction, to enhance stability, dig a trench about

Design and Cultivation It is possible to cultivate a succulent garden in less than ideal conditions, even in areas prone to freezing temperatures and rainy winters. Many cold hardy succulents thrive in regions that experience prolonged, hard frosts. When water freezes at 32°F (0°C), it expands which can burst plant cell walls and turn them to mush. Those succulents that are frost tolerant have salts in their cellular fluids that lower the temperature at which the fluid freezes, or they can handle the formation of ice within their cells. Non hardy succulents may survive freezing temperatures if their roots are unharmed. But unlike perennials that continually replenish their leaves, frost burned succulents may appear shriveled and blackened for months—even years. If this destroys the symmetrical shape and beauty of the plant, there may little point in trying to salvage it. The preferred temperature range for non hardy succulents is 40° to 85°F, but many will tolerate temperatures into the low 30s and highs in excess of 100°F (when grown in semi shade). Other ideal climate conditions include minimal rainfall (fewer than 20 inches per year) and low humidity (the drier, the better). If you live where temperatures occasionally dip below 32°F, but hard frosts are rare, you may be able to cultivate tender succulents in the ground year round— providing you cover the plants when frost threatens or grows them in your garden's warmer microclimates. A protected pocket can vary by several life saving degrees from an exposed area.

CHAPTER 2

Growing Succulents in Colder Climates

UNDERSTANDING MICROCLIMATES

because cold air is heavier than warm air, it flows downhill and pools in low spots. To identify these cold pockets in your garden that is notice where ice crystals linger the longest after sunrise. Warm spots tend to be near boulders, structures, trees, hard cape, and asphalt, which absorb heat from the sun during the day and release it gradually at night. Wind is a factor, too. Garden areas shielded by walls, hedges, or some other windbreak will be warmer than those out in the open. Locations exposed to northerly winds tend to be colder. But wind is not always a problem; air that moves is less of a threat than air that is still, because movement keeps cold air from settling around plants. Wind can make leaves more frost resistant, because it has a drying effect, and drier leaves contain less water. Good air circulation also discourages pests and fungal diseases, to which succulents are prone in damp climates. Excessive wind will cause desiccation, however, and if you are sheltering your plants within a cold frame, in a greenhouse, or beneath a cover, wind may cause greater heat loss by cooling the air around the structure. Your garden's warmest microclimate, and the best place to grow frost tender succulents in winter, is likely a sunny, south facing area— ideally a slope backed by a fence or retaining wall, protected by adjacent trees, and/or strewn with boulders.

HARD FROSTS AND WET WEATHER

if you live in zone 8 or below, the tender succulents growing in your garden likely will have to be replaced from one year to the next or brought indoors in autumn. If your succulents are potted, this makes the job easy—especially if large specimens are on wheeled stands or you have a dolly handy. Be sure to check plants for insects, snails, and other pests you do not want to keep warm and snug all winter. Another option is to take plant cuttings or divisions in autumn, root them indoors in pots or fl arts during the winter, and then introduce the young plants to your garden in spring. Small succulents also can be dug up—most can be uprooted easily—then potted and over wintered as houseplants. Regardless of where you live, one way to landscape your garden with no hardy succulents is to grow them in nursery pots submerged in the soil up to the rims. As first frost approaches, lift the pots out of the ground and bring them inside—ideally into a place where the plants will spend the winter beneath timed fluorescent lights. Succulents also can be over wintered in a greenhouse, providing it is well ventilated and the humidity is low. In spring, when you are ready to reintroduce the plants to the garden, acclimatize them gradually to outside temperatures and the sun's ultraviolet rays. Sunburn can cause permanent scarring, which is particularly a concern with

Succulents that are thin skinned or variegated. The best time to introduce your potted succulents to the outdoors is during mild, cloudy weather. Place them in bright shade, leave them there a few days, and then move them into partial— and finally, full—sun. Cacti and succulents that do best in dappled shade during the summer in the Southwest may prefer full sun in northern states, but keep in mind that low angled northern sun, at higher elevations, can be intense. Excessive rainfall also is a concern. Succulents grown for prolonged periods in soggy soils will rot. Evaluate your soil for its ability to drain well, and note which areas of your garden are likely to stay drier. Plant on slopes or atop mounds of soil amended with decomposed granite or pumice, and avoids planting in depressions or basins in which water collects. Also, remove decaying leaves that collect in the crowns of succulents and on the surrounding ground. (It is not water that causes rot, but fungus or bacteria in organic matter.) Mulch only with gravel or fast draining decomposed granite, and tent prized plants during rainstorms. COPING WITH OCCASIONAL FROST In my own garden (USDA climate zone 9), I cover vulnerable aeronauts, aloes, kalanchoes, and Agavattenuateta with bed sheets on those clear, still, midwinter nights during which frost is predicted. Like my neighbors who own citrus and avocado groves, I watch the news or check the Internet daily from November through March to see if a "frost advisory" has been issued, which means temperatures will drop into the low 30s late at night and become progressively colder until daybreak.. Do not use plastic, because it traps moisture and intensify as the heat of the morning sun—a combination that can be more harmful than a light frost. Also avoid any material heavier than a bed sheet, especially when covering soft leaved succulents; the weight of the fabric can break or crease leaves, causing permanent damage. Remove the fabric as soon as possible after sunrise so the plants can dry and trapped moisture can evaporate. You can create a temporary canopy with tree branches, too. Push the cut ends of branches into the soil, so that the leaves arch up and over the plants you want to protect. Remove the branches if the weather turns wet, as they will hold moisture and drop decaying leaves. Frost tender succulents also can be protected with cold frames or floating row covers. With the latter, arched, flexible poles create a tunnel over the plants. This in turn is covered with a lightweight fabric (sold by the roll at garden centers), which is translucent and porous, allowing sunlight to shine through and

Moisture and evaporate. Lay the material over the plants and secure the edges by weighing them with stones, bricks, or two by fours. If the forecast is for light frost night after night (temperatures may dip below freezing, but only briefly), and you do not want to bother covering and uncovering plants repeatedly, skirt them with fabric for the duration. The temperature inside the screen will stay higher than that of the surrounding air by several degrees, which may be all that is needed. Place ¼ inch diameter wood dowels, metal rods, or bamboo or redwood plant stakes at least 18 inches tall (taller, if you are protecting a big plant) in the ground at 2 foot intervals. Use clothespins to attach fabric to the rods as you wrap it around them, forming a vertical screen. This will create somewhat of a windbreak, too, but obviously will not stand up to high winds. It also may not prevent frost from burning the tips of the leaves. Winter weather that is most threatening to succulents is rain followed by frost, because plant cells are engorged with water. New growth is particularly vulnerable. Often—especially with aloes—the tips of pointed leaves freeze, but the rest of the plant is fine. These tips will remain dry and shriveled, which does not harm the plant but may compromise its appearance. Irrigate your tender succulents infrequently during the colder months to decrease their water content and increase the salt to water ratio of cellular fluid. Frost indicators When winter temperatures begin to dip into the 30s, be vigilant. All it takes is a few hours below freezing to cause lasting damage to tender succulents. Take measures to protect your plants when these conditions are evident: The air is still. There is no cloud cover. Stars glitter. Humidity is low. The moon is new or full. The soil is dry and cold. Daytime temperatures do not exceed 75°F. An arctic air mass or cold front impacts the area. The dew point (the temperature at which moisture in the air condenses into dew) is close to freezing

How Thomas Hobbs over winters his garden. Garden designer Thomas Hobbs of Vancouver, British Columbia, brings his garden's succulents indoors in October and replants them outdoors in March. This excerpt from The Jewel Box Garden (2004) offers his advice. ***The trend of gardening with masses of non-hardy succulents is limited by the fear of winter. What do you do with them then? They are too beautiful to be considered disposable. All they need is bright light and an above freezing windowsill to hang in there until spring. Lack of light in winter will result in stretched growth and very unattractive plants. Lower leaves will turn yellow, then papery and need constant removal. If you cannot provide a very bright location for winter storage of your succulents, give them to someone who can, or set up a grow light in the basement or an unused area. Keep the plants very close to the tubes if these are fluorescent, and watch for stretching. Gardeners with hundreds of Echeverias (they multiply like rabbits!) stash them in plastic flats, not pots. At my house, I call this "Operation Echeveria Lift." Around Halloween, helpers from my nursery come with our big truck and we begin scooping them up with our bare hands. We place them tightly beside each other in plastic nursery flats and spend the next month cleaning them up. We check for insect grubs, slugs and rot, then group the plants by variety and place them, root ball and all, in flats. They spend the winter in semi hibernation in a barely heated but bright greenhouse. They receive much less water (maybe once a week) and are allowed to rest. Around March 1, I begin fertilizing again. A liquid feed of 20 20 20 at half my usual strength wakes them up. The increased light that spring brings really turns these plants on! Struggling specimens suddenly perk up and look happy. Once all danger of frost has passed, I place the flats of Echeverias out in the sun to "harden off" for a month or so. This direct sun brings out the subtle coloring and individuality of each variety. Then it is time to play

INDOOR CULTIVATION

Succulents least likely to survive frost tend to be those that adapt best to indoor culture. Unlike cold tolerant succulents, non hardy succulents do not require a hard frost as part of their natural cycle, and they thrive in the same conditions that make humans comfortable. A minimum 10-degree difference in temperature between day and night will encourage flowering. Succulents grown as houseplants must have bright light. Position them beneath a skylight or near a window, making sure that sunlight magnified by window glass does not burn the leaves. Place pots a few feet away from the window, or cover the glass with a sheer curtain or translucent blind. Rotate the plants every few days, so they will grow upright. Succulents etiolate (lengthen and become spindly) as they stretch toward a light source, which compromises their geometric shapes. Avoid placing potted succulents near indoor spas, humidifiers, or showers that generate a lot of steam. Plants that stay damp are prone to mildew, and minimal air circulation makes leaves a breeding ground for pests such as mealy bugs. Cacti, in particular, need good air circulation; if possible, place them near windows that can be opened during the warmest hours of the day. Succulents do nicely on a sun porch, and if it has a stone, tile, or brick floor that cannot be damaged by spilled soil or water, so much the better. But potted succulents grown indoors during their winter dormancy do not require much water—once a week, to moisten the soil, is plenty. Let them go dry, or nearly so, between watering.

COLD CLIMATE SUCCULENTS

More than 50 varieties of Opuntia and more than a dozen varieties of Echinocereus cacti will grow where temperatures drop below zero—according to members of the Ottawa Cactus Club, who have grown and tested them in their gardens. For example, Mammillaria vivipara (syn. Coryphantha vivipara), a globular rock garden plant with white spines and showy purple pink flowers, is very hardy; it grows wild in Alberta, Canada, and as far south as Texas. A few large succulents will tolerate temperatures to zero and below. Among them are Yucca filamentosa, Y. flaccida, Y. glauca, Y. gloriosa, Y. harrimaniae, and Y. schottii; and Agave havardiana, A. lechuguilla, A. neomexicana, A. parryi, A. toumeyana, and A. utahensis. Aloe polyphylla, the only aloe that thrives in temperatures well below freezing, is one of the rarest. It is arguably the most beautiful aloe, because its green, triangular leaves form a flattened whorl that resembles a lavish bow. It is native to the high mountains of Lesotho, South Africa, and is in danger of extinction. It does not mind being buried beneath snow, but it must have exceptionally well-drained soil. Aloe polyphylla may never be common in the hot, dry Southwest, but

as it becomes more readily available, it likely will be a prized addition to gardens in colder climates. A yellow blooming variety reputed to be even more cold tolerant is D. nubigenum. Lewisia cotyledon (zones 6 through 10) is an alpine wild flower native to the Northwest. The genus was named after its discoverer, explorer Meriwether Lewis. Lewisia cotyledon prefers full sun to part shade in warm climates and well drained soil. Water minimally in winter or plants may rot. Lewisias belong to the Portulacaceae and like hot, dry summers. Plants produce daisylike white, pink, or apricot yellow flowers atop 12 inch burgundy red stems in spring and summer (year round along the Pacifi c coast). Lewisia cotyledon sold in nurseries include white and pink 'Siskiyou' varieties, which are hardy to zone 3, and L. rediviva, which is hardy in zones 4 through 8. Orostachys species are intriguing succulents for containers and rock gardens. Bright green rosettes about 2 inches in diameter elongate into tall, conical flower spikes in autumn. Plants are monocarpic (they die after flowering), but offsets take their place. Hardy to 32°F, they grow best in well drained soil in partial shade.

Rhodiola often is lumped with Sedum, but the former is a separate genus that includes about 50 species of fleshy perennials with rhizomatous roots. Many rhodiola resemble large sedums and form masses of plants with multiple stems covered with slender, often toothed leaves. Individual star shaped flowers bloom in cream, red, orange, or yellow. Most rhodiola originated in northern Europe, the Himalayas, Tibet, Afghanistan, Mongolia,

Or China and therefore thrive in colder parts of North America as well as

Canada. (They most often are seen in Pennsylvania, New York, Maine, and Vermont.) Among the most common is roseroot (R. rosea, zones 2 through 9), which produces tightly massed pink flowers on 12   inch stems in summer.

The roots smell like roses. Sedum (stonecrop), though naturalized in the United States, is native to Europe. Widely cultivated sedums that are cold tolerant and that, remarkably, will grow in most zones include the following fine leaved ground covers (2 to 5 inches): S. acre (goldmoss sedum), which has light green leaves and clusters of yellow flowers; S. album, which spreads readily and can be invasive; and S. anglicum, which has dark green leaves a mere V inch long. Shrublike sedums that grow to 18 inches tall, thrive in zones 5 through 10, and die to the ground in winter include Sedum spectabile, which has 3 inch long blue green leaves and domed flower clusters that come in a variety of colors; andS. telephium, which resembles S. spectabile but has narrower, gray green leaves. Both perennials die to the ground after flowering. Sedum rupestre 'Angelina' (Angelina stonecrop) (zones 7 through 10), forms a frilly mat of chartreuse and golden yellow leaves that turn rust red at the tips when stressed. Clusters of starry yellow flowers appear in summer. This versatile plant makes a great ground cover and is striking when massed. Use it to create rivers of color amid fl owerbeds, as a border, and in juxtaposition with plants with deep red flowers and foliage. It is also lovely cascading from a container or tucked into a stone wall. Sedum spurium is a ground hugging succulent with dark green or bronzy leaves about an inch long; it spreads to 2 feet or more. In late summer, dome shaped flower clusters appear and mature into pink flowers. Sedum spurium 'Dragon's Blood' has purple bronze leaves and burgundy blooms; S. spurium 'Tricolor' is variegated green, cream, and rosy pink; and S. spurium 'Bronze Carpet' is a rich coppery green. All effectively add color to rock gardens, containers, and patterned plantings. Sempervivum, or houseleek, is perhaps the best known genus of the frost tolerant succulents. The plants commonly are called hen and chicks, because small offsets nestle around the mother plant. They are attached by slender stems; once the little plants root, they become independent.

Sempervivum arachnoideum (commonly called cobweb houseleek, zones 5 through 10) has pointed leaf tips webbed with white threads. These catch dew during spells of drought to keep the plant hydrated. Sempervivum is related to Jovibarba, a genus that looks similar but has bell shaped pale yellow flowers. Cultivation requirements are the same, except Jovibarba is less tolerant of prolonged wet conditions. Jovibarba hirta (also known in the nursery trade as Sempervivum hirta) and J. sobolifera (S. sobolifera) are native to the Soviet Union and are exceptionally cold tolerant.

CHAPTER 3

Plant Care and Propagation

Succulent gardens require much less care than lawns, fl owerbeds, and pruned hedges. However, all plants are living things and change over time. As your garden's artistic director, you have the job—and, hopefully, pleasure—to make sure those changes happen when, where, and how you want them. Keeps your garden looking good year round with minimal effort with the following practical methods for planting and grooming, controlling weeds and pests, and propagating plants? IN GROUND PLANTING TIPS Prior to planting, spade compacted soil to loosen it, so roots will penetrate easily. When transplanting a succulent from its nursery pot, dig a whole deep enough to cover its roots, once they have been freed from the pot and untangled. Elevate the crown slightly to compensate for sinking later on. As soon as the plant is situated, tamp the dirt around its base, and then water well to settle the roots. (If a succulent has yet to establish roots or is dormant, withhold water for several weeks to prevent rotting.) When planting nursery flats of succulent ground covers, use a trowel to dig holes several inches deep and about a foot apart. Separate the plants, insert one into each hole, and press the loose soil gently around the roots to anchor them. Succulents that are large (several feet high and equally wide) can be surprisingly heavy. Lifting and moving them is a two person job, even with the help of a dolly or wheeled cart. When working with any large spiny or prickly plant, wear elbow length leather gloves and eye protection. Professional landscapers, when transporting "armed and dangerous" succulents, wrap them in carpet remnants—which protects the plants as well as the people. When planting a small cactus, wrap it with a towel folded so that you can lift the plant with the ends, or simply hold it with kitchen tongs. Basketball sized spherical cacti, such as golden barrels (Echinocactus grissini), can be moved by rolling them onto a beach towel, which serves as a sling. Larger cacti, though highly desirable, are much more challenging to relocate. The safest and most efficient way is to carry the plant on a stretcher—not the kind used to transport injured people, but one constructed of rigid boards that can support the plant's weight. Though it takes two to lift it, a stretcher is better than a wheelbarrow, because it can be placed on the ground next to the plant, which is rolled onto it. To lift a large cactus, lasso it with a rope thick enough (at least an inch in diameter) not to cut the plant's flesh. When the plant is in position, use the rope to hold it while a helper fills in the soil in the planting hole beneath it. Give newly transplanted cacti four to six weeks to settle in before watering them. WEED CONTROL Spring brings abundant growth. Plants that have been dormant all winter produce new leaves, flowers, and eventually seeds. Unfortunately, when garden plants are at their most lush, so are weeds. What begins as a few green sprouts ends up a dense thicket that rapidly goes to seed to ensure its survival the following year? But weeds must be removed; they compromise the beauty of the garden and rob prized plants of sunlight, water, and nutrients. Weeds tend to be more of a problem wherever soil is exposed, because seeds need sun to germinate. Succulent ground covers work well to keep weeds under control, but they take time to fill in. Until they do, the best way to deprive weed seeds of sunlight is to mulch bare ground. You can do this with shredded bark, pebbles, gravel, or decomposed granite—whatever looks natural and is best suited to your climate and terrain. (Bear in mind that organic mulches generally are not the best choice for cacti and succulents.) Those few weeds that sprout in mulch are easy to pull, because their roots are not cemented into hard soil. I do not have much of a weed problem in my half acre garden, even in exposed areas and dirt pathways, because I deal with weeds six months before they sprout. I sprinkle a powdered preemergent herbicide (which prevents seeds from germinating) on any bare spots, including pathways. This is one of the few garden chemicals that I find essential. I buy a 25 pound sack of preemergent from a nursery or agricultural supplier in December—earlier, if rain is forecast— and spread it wherever I do not want to pull weeds, come spring. The downside is that no seeds from desirable plants will germinate in those areas, but I believe that is a small sacrifice. What should you do if you have not spread preemergent herbicide, and spring is fast approaching? Be vigilant, and hoe the soil as soon as you see uninvited slivers of green. At that point, weeds are young, tender, and lightly rooted. In areas where a hoe is too large, you can disturb the soil with a trowel or even a steel file or spackling knife. This may seem tedious, but the larger a weed gets, the more difficult it will be to remove. If weeds are growing amid cactus or other spiny plants, and it is impossible to pull those weeds without injuring yourself, use a long, slender brush to paint as many weed leaves as you can reach with glyphosate (one commercial brand Is Roundup). Do not spray the herbicide if some may land on your prized plants. Contrary to wishful thinking, glyphosate does indeed harm succulents and cacti. If weeds have gotten away from you, and the task of eliminating them seems overwhelming, at least do the minimum: Remove any flower buds or seed heads. This is more important than uprooting the plant, which you can do later or simply let it die at the end of its annual growth cycle. (In fact, if erosion is a concern, roots of annual weeds should be left in the soil.) The urgent need is to prevent weeds from setting seed, because once they do, you will have to contend with their numerous offspring the following year. Be sure to bag all weeds and send them out with the trash. Do not leave them lying on the ground or add them to your compost pile.

GROOMING YOUR PLANTS

remove any dirt and leaves that have fallen onto the crowns of rosette succulents to keep them tidy and prevent moisture accumulation that may cause tissue damage. An occasional blast with the jet setting of a pistol sprayer works nicely. If rainfall is minimal in your area, hose down all your succulents from time to time; a good cleaning will diminish pests as well as dust. Aloes, aeronauts, agaves, yuccas, and other succulents send up long lasting bloom spikes that are a joy to behold, but eventually they become unsightly as the blooms fade. When deadheading, cut the stalk where it emerges from the plant. Of course, the entire plant also will need to be removed if it dies after flowering. A few succulents, particularly senesces, have insignificant cant blooms that, to me, look messy and should be removed. On the other hand, two that delight me are snipped and discarded by other gardeners: the minaret like spires that elongate Kalanchoes Lucia and Crassula coccinea 'Campfi re'. These stretch the plants and eventually ruin them—but not if you sever the budding stems as they form. (This does not work with monocarpic plants such as agaves and aeronauts; once the plants gear up for flowering, they die regardless.) Aconitum trunks tend to look a bit naked when they reach 12 inches high or more. Snap off the rosettes several inches below the foliage, allow the cuttings to callus, and then replant; they will root readily. Either uproot and discard the gangly trunks, or wait to see if they report multiple branches—they often do, but not always. If agaves are growing near a path or anywhere their sharp terminal spines might pose a danger, you can snip the thorny tips (about ¼ inch) off the leaves without detracting from the symmetry of the plant. Should you need to remove an agave leaf that is damaged or encroaching on a walkway, cut it off as close to the trunk as possible. Try to avoid partially removing a leaf from any succulent; the blunted end will call attention to it and diminish the beauty of the plant. Some succulents, notably aloes, have lower leaves that curve downward, remaining on their stems. These dry leaves provide protection from sunburn and frost, so if those are concerns, keep the leaves; otherwise, if you find them unsightly, peel them away. Watch for pups that sprout near aloes and agaves. Remove them if they encroach where they are not wanted, and replant them where they are. HAIL AND SNAILS Two of the most damaging things that can befall succulents growing out in the open happen to rhyme. There is nothing you can do about hail, unfortunately, because it is sudden and unpredictable. In a matter of seconds, it pockmarks succulent leaves— soft leaved agaves are particularly susceptible—giving them a freckled look. These blemishes do not go away, and since leaves on succulents can persist for several years, hail damage is truly unfortunate.

Snails cause long lasting and unsightly damage, too—sometimes latching onto a leaf and eating a whole right through it. Or they will eat their way across a leaf, leaving a scar. When they nibble black Aconitum arboretum 'Zwartkop', it looks sadly frayed, its exposed tissue white against the dark foliage. To tidy a snail bitten aeonium, remove damaged leaves by pinching them where they join the stem. Snails are insidious. During the day, they sleep in leaf litter or on the undersides of leaves. At night and on drizzly days, they emerge to eat their fill. Of the several snail solutions, none is ideal. You can hand pick them, but this means extreme vigilance, or their population will explode before you know it. You may not think you have a snail problem in March, but by mid April, you will find them everywhere. So start early, and look for young ones. By the time they are as big as your thumbnail, they are large enough to lay eggs. I simply step on them, but if you are squeamish, don latex gloves, gather snails in a trash bag, and tightly tie the top. Another approach is to spread a granular poison that kills snails. This is a concern if you have pets, and even "pet safe" brands may harm songbirds and beneficial insects. Moreover, snail bait is expensive, and it has to be reapplied continually. Do not assume you can spread snail bait once in April and the job is done. Four to six weeks later, the snails will resurge, and you will be back at the store, buying more.

I do not recommend using barriers to keep snails out, except copper bands on tree trunks; nor do I advocate placing shallow bowls of beer in the garden. However, if you provide snails with a dark, damp, cakelike shelter—such as an overturned clay pot—they will go into it. This is satisfying, until you realize the dozen or so in the pot represent a tiny percent of your garden's population. Geese eat snails, but I figure a large bird in my garden would cause more problems than it solves. What works best for me is, I regret to say, not an option for everyone. I release beneficial decollate snails throughout my garden (about one decollate snail per square foot). They do not nibble the leaves of healthy plants but rather feed on decaying matter, and—more importantly— the eggs and young of brown helix snails. Decollates have conical shells and are about an inch long. They are not inexpensive, but in the long run, they cost less than snail bait. They also are a natural rather than a chemical solution. The downside is that it takes a while for decollates to get established, during which time helix snails continue to do irreversible damage. Moreover, you still have to hand picked mature helix snails; the alternative is to wait for them to die a natural death. Six weeks before releasing decollate snails; reduce the helix snail population by spreading snail bait. Never spread snail bait once you have introduced decollates. I reintroduce decollates during every winter rainy season, because their population seems to wane—perhaps they have been preyed upon by birds or rodents, or they move on. Helix snails, on the other hand, need no assistance reintroducing themselves. Decollates are approved in some parts of the country, but not in others, for fear they will disrupt the ecological balance. Not that much seems to be in balance anymore; helix snails, for example, are not native. Their origin is shrouded in the murk of history, but one theory is that they were introduced as a potential food source. Indeed, that is the only control measure I have yet to try. HARMFUL INSECTS just when I have led you to the conclusion that the only answer to keeping your succulents beautiful is to grow them indoors let me caution you about mealy bugs and scale. Plants that do not receive good air circulation and that grow in a humid environment are prone to sucking insects. Succulents in the garden also attract aphids or trips when flowering buds are young and tender. Mealy bugs look like bits of cotton fluff; scale are hard, oval brown bumps; and aphids and trips are pinhead sized, soft bodied insects that chew and destroy new tissue. Mealy bugs usually can be spotted in leaf axils, but they sometimes attach themselves to roots. Scale, on the other hand, tends to latch onto stems and the underside of leaves. Plants with a severe mealy bug or scale infestation should be destroyed, lest the pests spread to healthy plants. Discard the soil and wash the pot thoroughly before reusing it. Plant Care and

Insecticides can be sprayed on mealy bugs, trips, scale, and other pesky insects, but I simply use rubbing alcohol instead. I keep it handy in a spray bottle, ready to go at the first sign of a problem. A fine, light spray of alcohol does no damage to succulent leaves and kills the bugs instantly. Aloes are prone to aloe mite, a microscopic insect that causes tissues near the stem to grow lumpy and distorted. Unfortunately, no cure is known, and affected plants or portions thereof must be removed and destroyed to prevent infestation of neighboring plants. Any tools that may have touched diseased tissue must be cleaned and disinfected. If your succulents are damaged by rot, you can try to salvage the plant by cutting out the damaged area and replanting the healthy tissue. During a record wet winter in my garden, the roots of a handsome clump of Aconitum 'Sunburst' succumbed to rot. At first, the tops of the plants seemed fine, but the florets gradually shrank in size, until what was a lush mini forest looked wan and spindly. When I pressed the stems, they were firm at the top and soft at the bottom. I pulled the entire clump from the soil, discarded the decayed tissue, and cut the stems to salvage the florets, retaining several firm, healthy inches. The cuttings since have rooted and are thriving. Cotyledon buds, damaged by aphids, may not open.

PROPAGATION

The majority of succulents are winter dormant, so the best time to propagate them is in spring, as they begin their active growth cycle and before summer heat intensify as. Autumn is the best time to start summer dormant succulents, such as aeronauts, haworthias, sempervivums, and senesces. Get new plants off to a good start in pots or flats. Any commercial cactus mix will do, but you can make your own. The Huntington Botanical Gardens formula is two parts forest humus, two parts pumice, one part builders' sand, plus trace amounts of superphosphate and cottonseed meal. Place pots and flats in a warm, sheltered nursery area of your garden that receives bright light but no full sun during the hottest part of the day. When young plants are well rooted, you can transplant them into the garden. Once in the ground, for the first week or so, they should be protected from harsh sun; shade them with empty nursery flats or dry, twiggy tree branches. Or simply move a piece of garden furniture so it is between plants and sun at midday. Mulch with gravel to help cool the soil surface and slow evaporation. At the base of the slender, gel filled leaves of Bulbine frutescens is a stem along which grow spaghetti shaped tuberous roots. These are either in the ground, partially exposed, or entirely exposed, depending on how friable and moist the soil is. (If the ground is dry and hard, the plant's runners tend to be more accessible.) To propagate B. frutescens, dig a trench several inches deep and a foot or so long Lay one or two rhizomatous stems into it and cover with soil, with leaves exposed. Propagation in commercial nurseries and at botanical gardens takes place in temperature controlled greenhouses, beneath fixtures that provide artificial sunlight. Professionals also have methods of collecting, labeling, storing, and germinating seeds, and they follow prescribed schedules for repotting plants in

Successively larger containers. Since most of this is beyond what home gardeners are willing or able to do, the methods described here are most useful for the novice. Keep in mind that perhaps more than any other type of plant, succulents are easy to propagate. More often than not, if you study the plant, how it reproduces will become obvious. Cuttings Propagation by cuttings is a process that needs no special skill or tools. If you have started geraniums from cuttings, you know how to propagate succulents with stems. Cleanly cut several inches of stem with leaves attached, using garden shears, scissors, or a sharp knife. The stem should have at least two nodes (the thickened area where leaves emerge): one to produce roots, the other for leaves. Because the cut end is raw and open, give it several days to heal—the tissue that forms over the end is called callus. Although some books recommend dipping stems into sculpture to discourage fungus or in rooting hormone to promote cellular growth, I do not bother. If you delay planting the cuttings, after a week or so, roots may grow anyway— into thin air. Succulents are able to reverse the flow of growth, sending nutrients from stems and leaves into root formation. As this happens, leaves will shrivel, but as soon as new roots take hold, leaves will plump and the plant will thrive. Some succulents, notably Aconitum haworthias, form whiskery aerial roots along the undersides of stems. These are attempting to connect with the soil, so all you have to do is help them. Dig a shallow trench and lay the stem in it, root side down; then cover with dirt. Fat leaved graptopetalums, pachyphytums, and some non hybrid echeverias will form roots and even tiny new plants at the base of dropped leaves. To encourage this, rest the leaf, stem end down, atop potting soil. Keep soil moist but not soggy; mother leaves and their offspring tend to rot easily. Remember that when handling cuttings from euphorbias, you should wear gloves and eye protection; the milky sap is caustic. Division

Uprooting (or unpotting) an overgrown clump and pulling the stems and roots apart is called division. Sometimes roots are so dense and tangled they have to be sawn apart—which often is the case with overgrown sansevierias. Divide offsets by cutting or wiggling them loose from the parent, and then peel away any old, dry leaves. When you plant the offspring, space them so they will have room to reproduce on their own. Rhizomes are fleshy underground roots from which new plants sprout. These pups are a bonus if you want them and a nuisance if you do not. In any case, propagation is easy: simply dig up the new plant and it is ready to replant else where. Agave Americana launches vigorous rhizomes laterally under the soil, which soon results in a cluster of smaller pups nestled at its base. I have seen A. Americana pups pop up several feet from the mother plant, which seems to look demurely the other way, as though to say, "Those are not mine!" I made the mistake of planting Aloe sayonara in my succulent tapestry, which has a geometric arrangement. Now that the succulents in the tapestry have filled in, I do very little weeding, except to remove A. sayonara pups growing where I do not want them. The soil in the bed is loose and sandy, so I grab the pup firmly at its base and lift up. This exposes a rhizome about ½ inches thick, which, like an umbilical cord, connects the young plant to its mother. I cut the rhizome at the base of the parent plant and discard the offspring. Bulbils and plantlets Bulbils are tiny plants that grow along bloom spikes. Perhaps the most dramatic examples are agaves and furcraeas that literally pump their life force into tall, multi flowered stalks. After each flower drops its petals, its base (ovary) swells

And produces leaves, creating one of many tiny replicas of the mother. The parent plant's demise continues to help the propagation process; when it collapses and the flower spike falls, it propels hundreds of young plants onto the ground. Some smaller succulents, such as Haworthias attenuate and ground cover Crassula multivalve, also produce new plants on the tips of flower spikes. When this slender stalk gets heavy, it lowers its burden to the soil, where the young plant—which by then may have sprouted roots—takes hold. Kalanchoes in the Bryophyllum genus form plantlets along their scalloped leaf margins, giving them a ruffled look; these drop by the dozens and take root. Some gardeners consider such abundance a nuisance, and indeed it can be. On the plus side, if these young plants are allowed to mature, they produce lovely parasols of bell shaped flowers. Beheading Leggy aeronauts and showy hybrid echeverias—those that resemble ruffle ed cabbages—are best propagated by having their "heads" cut off. This sounds drastic, but it is easy to do and rewarding. As the plant grows, its stem elongates, which is not as attractive as a tight rosette with no stem showing. When you tire of looking at the ungainly stem, remove any shriveled leaves from the base of the rosette. With a sharp knife, slice horizontally through the stem, severing the rosette about an inch below its base. Place the rosette in a sheltered, shady area, ideally upright with its bottom leaves resting atop an empty pot. In ten days or so, the cut end will have callused and sprouted roots. Pot it in fresh soil. Do not discard the original plant's decapitated stem. Keep it in its pot and tend it as when it was intact. New rosettes may grow from one or more leaf axils. When these are 2 or 3 inches in diameter, remove and plant them.

CHAPTER 4

Conclusion

Succulent Diseases and Problems: Solutions to Your Plant's Symptoms

Succulents are desert plants so they do not need to be watered often. They still need watering though and the amount of watering they get is a delicate balance. Too much or too little will cause problems to set in, They are fairly responsive plants though so when you adjust the watering, many of the problems can be rectified within just a few hours.

Don't believe the myth that it's extremely hard to kill these hardy plants because without taking precautions to treat early signs that there's a problem with your plant, it can see them die a premature death.

Some of the questions listed below will help you identify the most common to the most pressing concerns about growing healthy succulents and treating problems before they become fatal.

Succulent Plant Diseases, Problems and the Solutions for Them!

Why is my succulent shriveling?

When you notice your plant begin to shrivel, check the leaf color and texture. If it's yellowing and shriveling, it's under watered and will feel dry to the touch. Yellowing leaves on a well-watered plant is too much water with a mushier feel to the leaves.

What Causes the Leaves on Succulents to Fall Off?

The leaves on your succulent will start to fall off if you continue to over water it. Yellowing happens first and is a sign of a watering issue – too much or not enough. There's a 50/50 chance you'll get it wrong and continue to over water it.

Now, growing succulents in soil needs the right potting mix. Like most plants, they need both water and nutrients, which the soil will retain for the plant to feed on when it needs it. Since succulent plants are better storing water and nutrients in the plant itself, the soil needs to drain faster than your average potting soil. Otherwise, the roots will continue to soak in the water and stay there because the rest of the plant will have no need for it.

The soil used should be labeled specifically for succulents or cacti plants to ensure you're getting a potting mix with better drainage.

If you still find the soil retaining too much water for too long, another thing you can do is put some pumice through the soil to assist in both aeration and water absorption.

Other options include adding:

- Perlite

- Sand

- Mulch

- Vermiculite

However, pumice is usually the preferred option to improve drainage, so use that first. If that doesn't improve it enough, the other options above could help too. Remember to start with the right type of potting soil. Potting mix for succulents and cacti plants, and then add your pumice to that for better aeration.

Why are my succulents turning brown?

Browning leaves on succulents are a warning sign that you're underwatering the plant. Along with that, you'll notice the leaves start shriveling.

Gradually increase the amount of water you give the plant and if you're using pumice in your soil, cut back on the amount used.

What's the white stuff growing on my plant?

There are a few things that can cause a white coating to cover the leaves of succulents. Only one is good and that's Epicuticular wax. This is a wax coating that will cover the entire surface of the plants leaves and should not be scrubbed off. It's there as a natural sun barrier to protect the plant.

That being said, it could also be something not so good. Other things that can cause white fungi to show on your plants include:

Powdery Mildew

This is a fungus that often starts on the underside of leaves before becoming visible on the top part. For that reason, when you're taking care of your plant, it's always a good idea to inspect under the leaves so you can catch this early. Although it is a fungal disease, it's rarely fatal. It will stunt the plant's growth though because with enough of it, photosynthesis will be impaired and leaves can start to fall off due the inability to feed on the right nutrients.

Mealy bug infestation

Mealy bugs are a succulent's worst enemy. When they're present, you'll notice white fluffy spots appearing on your plants. It'll start off with a few, but the female of the species can lie up to 600 eggs. Get a few of them and you'll soon see why they're a huge problem.

With enough of these, as in an infestation, the mealy bugs and the plants will be in battle for the water. With bugs in the hundreds or thousands, the plant has no chance. It'll eventually wither and die.

When dealing with a mealy bug infestation, don't rely on sprays. Use rubbing alcohol on a cotton swab and dab the insects rather than coating the leaves.

Are ants bad for succulents?

Sort of, they won't harm the plant directly, but they are a tell-tale sign that you have another insect problem because ants harvest aphids for their honeydew.

And that's not all. Another area of concern with ants is if they take up home in the soil. A colony of ants in the soil could destroy the root system so yeah, ants are bad for succulents.

The star attraction to ants is insects so if you're getting ants on your succulents, chances are there's another insect there that the ants are farming. Use sugar water to deter the ants and treat the main insect problem with a cotton swab and rubbing alcohol.

Why are the leaves on my succulent wilting/drooping?

Wilting/drooping is caused by insufficient water in the plant leaves. For succulents to stand upright, they need plenty of water in the leaves. When they start to droop, that's a sign you need to water them. The funny thing is that once you add more water, they'll pick up within just a few hours.

Why are there black spots on my succulents?

This could be sunburn, over watering, or perhaps even a bug problem. It's hard to tell so consider the growing conditions.

The most common cause is watering or using the wrong potting mix.

You can tell a lot from how the spot feels. If it's caused by sunburn, it'll be dry. If it feels mushy, it's too much water. If it's neither, then there's a chance it's a pest problem, in which case you can treat it with rubbing alcohol.

The black spots won't go away so just snip the leaf off (remember to sterilize your pruners).

One other thing to note is the type of plant affected by black spots. If it's a Jade plant, which is prone to developing black spots in the winter, the watering frequency needs altered because they don't grow in the winter. Also, the lighting conditions for plants grown indoors should be adapted to reflect the seasonal change to let the plant go into dormancy. Otherwise, the roots will take in more water than the leaves of the plant are going to use.

How to Revive a Succulent with Black Stem Rot

The most pressing of concerns with succulents is when you notice the stems are rotted. That can be fixed, so you don't need to toss the plant and start again. All you need is your trusted pruners to cut away the rotted part of the stem.

The fix for black stem rot is to repot the plant. When you do, there are a few things to pay attention to:

- That you use the right potting mix

- That the pot you use has drainage holes

- That you add enough pumice, gravel, sand, mulch, Perlite or any other substance to increase aeration and water absorption

- That the roots are not root-bound, meaning that if the roots have grown compacted, aeration could be decreased, in which case, you'll need to separate the roots to increase air flow before repotting

In Conclusion

While succulent plants are hardy plants that are relatively easy to care for, problems can set in if you don't understand what the plant is trying to tell you. They have their subtle ways of speaking to you to tell you what they need. They'll wilt when they need watered, and they'll swell when there's too much. Black spots and browning can occur if the root system takes in more water than the plant needs, which is why they do not need to be watered frequently. Even once a week on some types of succulents can be too much.